LIFE LESSONS

FROM A SLOTH

PAINT

**SARAH HENEGHAN, ALANA MILLS,
AND MADELINE STURGEON**

A POST HILL PRESS BOOK

Life Lessons from a Sloth
© 2018 by Post Hill Press
All Rights Reserved

ISBN: 978-1-68261-723-6

Cover and interior art by Darwin Marfil
Cover layout by Tricia Principe, principedesign.com
Interior Design and Composition by Greg Johnson/Textbook Perfect

Post Hill Press
New York • Nashville
posthillpress.com

Published in the United States of America
Printed in Canada

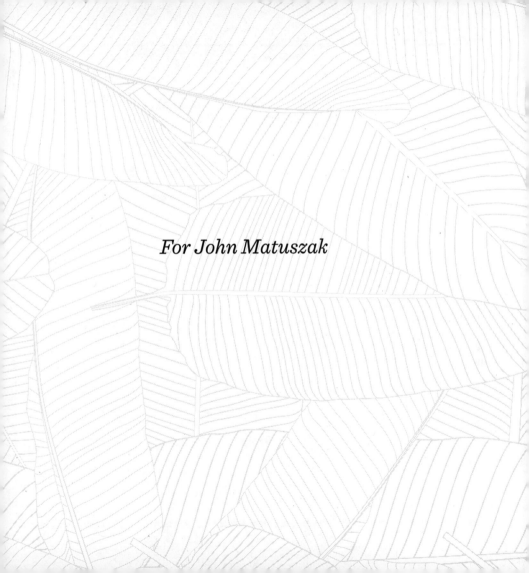

For John Matuszak

Introduction

This book features the six extant species of sloths:

- Brown-throated three-toed sloth
- Pale-throated three-toed sloth
- Pygmy three-toed sloth
- Maned three-toed sloth
- Linnaeus's two-toed sloth
- Hoffmann's two-toed sloth

Three-toed sloths have much longer arms than legs, have flat faces, and have three claws. They are probably what you think of when you imagine a sloth!

Two-toed sloths, meanwhile, have proportional arms and legs, slightly extended snouts, and two claws.

Each of these species has their own unique differences, but they all make up the wondrous world of sloths!

Explore new possibilities. You never know what might interest you! Like, for example, sloths.

Sloth Fact

According to experts at Costa Rica's sloth sanctuary, sloths are curious creatures.

A varied diet is important.
Eat that beetle. Do it!

Sloth Fact

While sloths are primarily vegetarian, they will occasionally eat insects, or even small rodents or birds.

Doing nothing with your friends can be just as fun as doing *something*.

Take good care of your claws,
I mean, nails.

Inhale. Exhale. Feel the tension evaporate. Practice your breathing for when times get tough.

Sloth Fact

Sloths respire slowly. Some can even hold their breath for forty minutes underwater!

When you are interested in someone, let them know!

Sloth Fact

Female three-toed sloths emit a loud, high-pitched scream at their prospective mating partners.

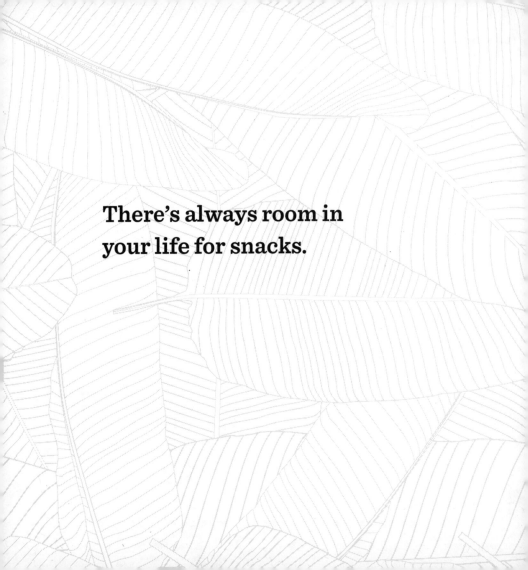

There's always room in your life for snacks.

Practice good hygiene!
You don't want to smell like
anything other than algae,
do you? ... That's a human
thing too, right?

Sloth Fact

*Sloths groom themselves at least once
per day. They also don't sweat, so they
have no body odor!*

It's okay to enjoy being alone!
Sometimes solitude is good
for relaxation.

Don't be afraid to show your playful side.

Sloth Fact

According to experts at the sloth sanctuary, sloths have a playful side that people rarely see.

Be resilient.
You can survive a fall.

Sloth Fact

Sloths are surprisingly sturdy animals, and are able to survive falls from the canopy.

Spend time outside in the sun
to help kickstart your day.

Sloth Fact

*Sloths are unable to shiver, so instead they
bask in the sun to warm themselves.*

If life seems bleak, nap!
Things will look better
in the morning.

Embrace your individual style!

Always take the time to splash in puddles.

Sloth Fact

Sloths will sometimes leave their trees to play in puddles on the forest floor.

It's good to have a full belly.

You are charming just as you are.

Mind your own business.

The body wants what the body wants. Usually, it's more sleep.

Claim your homestead.

**Every body is a weird body.
Rock what you are made of!**

There's safety in slowness.

Sloth Fact

Sloths move through the trees at about nine feet per minute, but only six feet per minute on the ground.

Respect others' tastes and preferences. To each their own!

Sloth Fact

Individual sloths tend to prefer a specific type of leaf above all others.

Know when to move on.
Don't let stress stick to you,
only moss.

Be one with nature. Literally.

Sloth Fact

Sloths are an important habitat for mosses and algae, which grow on their fur.

Avoid conflict, but when you can't, use your claws!

Never stop smiling!

Sloth Fact

Three-toed sloths are unable to change their facial expression.

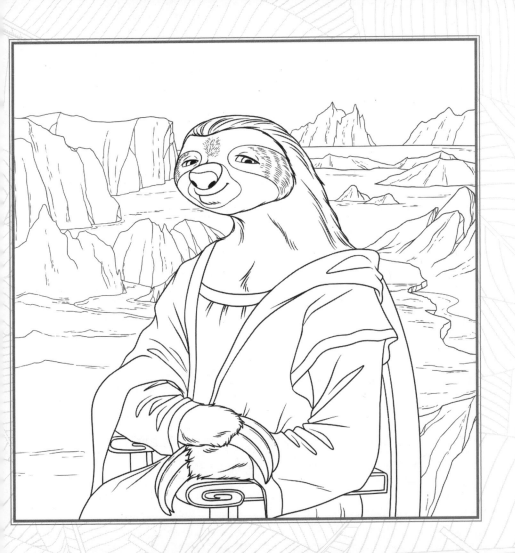

Swimming is an underrated workout.

Sloth Fact

Sloths can move three times faster in the water than they can on land.

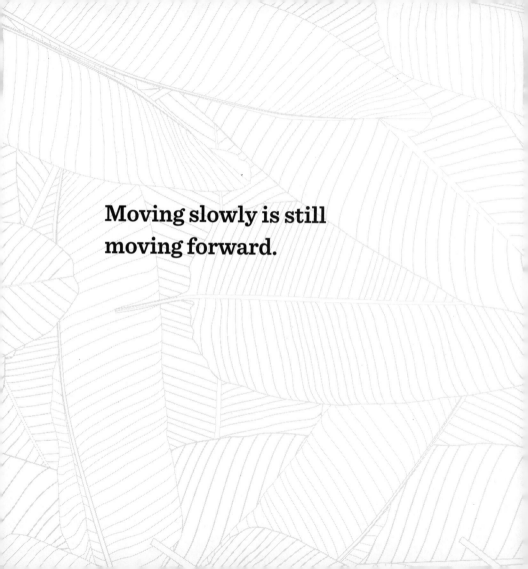

Moving slowly is still
moving forward.

Anything you can do today, can be done tomorrow. Take a nap!

Sloth Fact

Sloths sleep for eight to twelve hours in the wild, but up to eighteen hours in captivity!

Fresh food is the best food.

Sometimes it's not worth it to pick things back up after you've dropped them.

Find places and friends who make you feel safe.

Sloth Fact

Sloths sleep longer when they feel safe in their environment.

Practice your photo face!

Everyone sees the world differently. Be open to fresh perspectives.

Sloth Fact

Sloths spend much of their life hanging upside down.

Adapt to your environment, whatever that may be.

Sloth Fact

The moss and algae that grow on sloths provide important camouflage.

**Hold yourself together!
Maintain your composure
in times of crisis.**

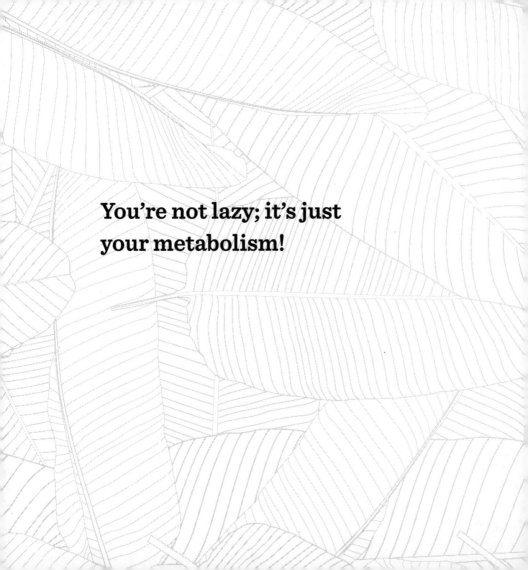

You're not lazy; it's just
your metabolism!

**Appreciate your parents,
and later your own children,
while you are together.**

Sloth Fact

*Baby sloths can remain with their mothers
for three to four years.*

Get out of your comfort zone, at least once a week.

Sloth Fact

Sloths descend to the forest floor to poop only once a week. Two-toed sloths descend from trees head-first, while three-toed sloths do not.

Make sure to eat your greens!

Don't rush through life.
Enjoy the journey.

Take care of your friends,
and they'll take care of you.

Sloth Fact

Sloths have a symbiotic relationship not only with plants, but moths as well.

There's a lot of sloths out there,
but there's only one you.

Sloth Fact

*Sloths are the most common mammal
in South America.*

Never let go. Seriously. *Never*.

Give your children your best tree.

Always consider the best use
of your time…

Go to a party, or take a nap?
Take a nap!

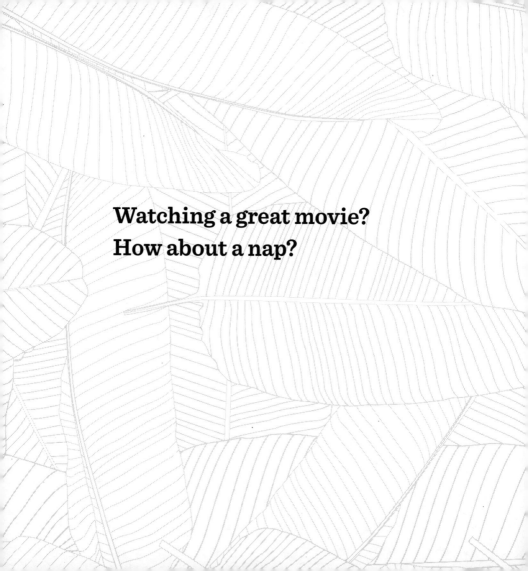

Watching a great movie?
How about a nap?

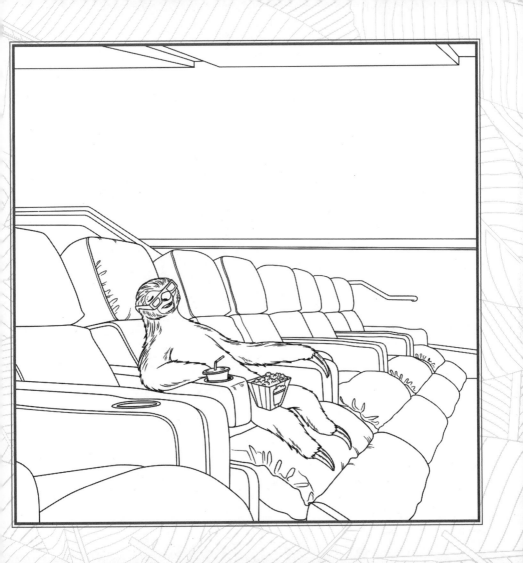

Cancelled plans? Nap! Better yet, cancel your plans and nap instead.

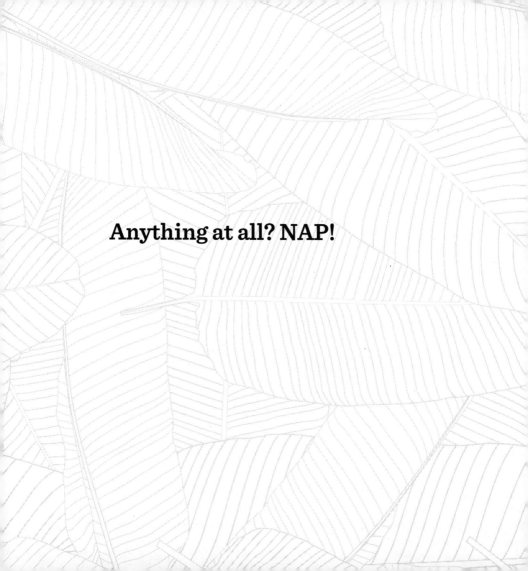

Anything at all? NAP!

Acknowledgments

We would first like to thank everyone who is involved in sloth research and conservation. Without them, this project could not exist.

To Michael Wilson, Anthony Ziccardi, and the digital and production teams at Post Hill Press: Thank you for your hard work in putting this book together! A special shout-out to Devon Brown, publicist extradionaire, for her efforts as well!

A huge thanks to Darwin for his wonderfully quirky illustrations, and to Greg and Tricia for their unparalleled design.

And, finally, we'd like to thank mammalogist Steve Sullivan at Miami University for his work in fact-checking, so that our silly sloth book is a silly, *accurate* sloth book.

About the Slothors

Sarah Heneghan is an avid bread- and pastry-baker, an amateur Assyriologist, and a 70s–80s pop music enthusiast. She is currently raising a sourdough starter named Henry on her kitchen counter. Though she remains a Chicagoan at heart, Sarah currently lives in Nashville with her husband and their two cats.

You can follow Sarah's cats on Instagram, @cricket_and_the_moose, or visit her website at sarah-heneghan.com.

Alana Mills is a coffee addict and arts enthusiast who only recently discovered her love of sloths, and now she is *obsessed*. She spent the first 18 years of her life in the sunny deserts of Southern California until she moved all the way across the country to go to school in North Carolina. When not working in the publishing world, she enjoys old school 35mm film photography, wrangling her uncooperative papillons, and traveling to see Renaissance art in its natural habitat.

Despite her lack of musical talent, she currently lives in Nashville TN with her two dogs, where she is still on the hunt for authentic Mexican food and the perfect brunch.

Madeline Sturgeon is a journalism and psychology graduate who now spends her days in the world of book publishing. She loves poetry, sweet tea, true-crime documentaries, and swimming in deep water. She currently resides in Nashville, but has lived all over the world, and misses Dublin and Chicago in particular.